TANTIVY

New Poems by Donald Revell

TANTIVY

Alice James Books
FARMINGTON, MAINE

10 9 8 7 6 5 4 3 2 1

Alice James Books are published by Alice James Poetry Cooperative, Inc., an
affiliate of the University of Maine at Farmington.

Alice James Books
238 Main Street
Farmington, ME 04938
www.alicejamesbooks.org

Library of Congress Cataloging-in-Publication Data
Revell, Donald
Tantivy / by Donald Revell.
  p. cm.
ISBN 978–1–882295–97–5 (pbk. : alk. paper)
I. Title.
PS3568.E793T36 2012
811'.54—dc23   2012018222

Alice James Books gratefully acknowledges support from individual donors,
private foundations, the University of Maine at Farmington, and the National
Endowment for the Arts.

ART WORKS.
arts.gov

COVER ART: *Sundown,* 1988 by Jane Freilicher. Currier Museum of Art,
Manchester, New Hampshire. Gift of Helen Burroughs Stern in Honor of
Gordon Smith, 1996.6

Contents

III. TITHON

IV. THE AFTERLIFE

Acknowledgments

My thanks go to the editors of the following journals where many of these poems, sometimes under different titles, originally appeared.

American Poet: "City"
The American Poetry Review: "Victorians," "Alsace," "Winter Solstice," "Moonlit cedar bursts in pain...," "Mornings on a twig...," "Out to the west..." and "Tithon"
Ancora Imparo: "Pigeon dying in the box..."
The Associative Press: "Barking Dogs"
Fawlt Magazine: "Victorians (11)"
Fifth Wednesday Journal: "True Love"
Barrow Street: "Aubade at the End," "Rapture" and "You are the color not made..."
Blackbox Manifold (UK): "Providence" and "Jules Laforgue writes to say..."
Columbia Poetry Review: "A line of hills..."
The Harvard Advocate: "Fedoras," "Pretty Alcoves" and "Faust cannot..."
Marsh Hawk Review: "Pure"
The Massachusetts Review: "Victorians (3)" and "Called"
Meridian: "The sky has slipped behind the moon..."
The Nation: "Victorians (10)"
New American Writing: "What the Colors Mean" and "Made Mention"
Poetry: "Homage to John Frederick Peto," "Birds small enough...," "Unreal precision of the houses..." and "Some motionless conflict in the sky..."
Sugar House Review: "Talons"
Volt: "Forgiving Bells"
Web Conjunctions: "Last Man"

Let me go: take back thy gift...

— TENNYSON

I

THE LAST MEN

Victorians

There is snow and there is snow.
A young woman, daughter of the eminent physician,
Disrobes at her window, and starvation,
Like a pack of dogs with jeweled mouths,
Pauses a moment, howls, and the young woman
Recites a poem to herself.

So long ago the words are lost
Even as each remains a part of us.
Christmas meaning snow out of a broiling sun.
Humanity meaning numbers.
Childhood meaning children and railings and kisses
Never kissed but carved into real trees.

Motherless goddamn modernity never grew.
Here we are again at Christmas
On fire escapes without a fire in view.

Victorians (2)

Carried thy lovely wail away to the window
A famous book with Alice in it and beasts
So much like ourselves they are us

Many small gods exhausted but still climbing
The word *snow* whispered among them and one
Girl imprisoned on the mountaintop growing old
In the new way in a transparency of white flowers
Painted onto white porcelain and bleeding

If there were a peril to run from I would run
There is a lion at the door and I see through him
Children teasing the small gods and clouds coming
Filled with the snow not one of them believes

I see the resurrection but two not one
Two white flowers breaking their hearts open

Victorians (3)

If I tell you the sun is happy in its work,
I've told you only the open secret of each day.
The day is not ours. We have no eyes for it.
And so the sun is happy.

Just to please me
Calendar says to long hair, "Rain."
Window says, "Rain,"
And window knows that calendar's a liar.

Frank O'Hara lives.
The tall grasses are perfectly
Ranged across Long Island.

I drink to the only two poems standing in the grass:
"Dover Beach" and O'Hara's
True account of talking to the sun…

Blindness has pinned a jeweled bicycle to the road.
If I tell you that the bicycle belongs to God,
I've told you only God is alive.
Goodbye is not a word.

Victorians (4)

Weather we knew, not seasons,
And of death fearing death itself
Beside a broken wineglass we knew only
There is snow and there is snow.

Angels underneath the Earth
Beat their luminous wings in vain.
In the concerned sky above us
Others pretend to bravery.

Science and faith left not a morsel
Of Shelley's heart clean for eating.
Weight of snow or weight of fruit,
The orchard dares not feed upon itself.

When at last I went outdoors—
Plants, ferns, distances—
Free birds had picked up all the dirt.
The broken trees had all been mended.

Victorians (5)

A ladybug scent of grass and the first irises
As if God had somehow reconciled the means
Of goodness to one pure instance of the good
South wind gentle rivulet calm sweep

I walk reciting every quiet word I know...

Mice are fast
Walls in Carcassonne
Are very fast horses
Owed much

The fossil record quietly accounts for me...

There is a sleep no man has ever known
There is an ocean of white laundry in Venice
A jonquil in India loud millions shut lily
Lucifer chrysolite Labrador the sun
Never yet touched a mountaintop
Where deer

Victorians (6)

A nothingness coated with ice
A pallid matrix but friendly
Wafer of light whiff of the Ganges
These mysteries must suffice
In the absence of Mystery

As the pillowed head in my dark bedroom might be anyone...

The distance fills and nearness is a void
Definition of empire
Outline of the pointillist afterlife where
Middens of ambulance mattresses and grasses
Welcome the roaring boys

As even one angel all alone is an Host and Eden...

I knew an early phantom of cold light called faith
I am a restless ape

Victorians (7)

An inadvertent crucifix of wildflowers
Found on pavement
Stands for the stillborn array
Unusual and usual animals

The baby's brow is kingly
Whose grave survives the grief

Christ drew each of us a circle
A birthplace with circumference
And from every limb and face
Fast serenity goes

I am also an arc
Of certainty and plumes
I never lived I never stayed
In the spellbound grassy world
Nor did you

Victorians (8)

Leave us for light the halo of your hair
And lilies asleep, occult, withheld, untrod
You were the lost signal from God
Undressed everywhere

Like a picture of hillsides that never existed
Green running up towards ramparts and down
To the quiet river whose white bed
Was a cloud

Very well I say
Nuptial change
The light thrilling
After you've gone

I see a very narrow path between water and fire
I see a killing cloud

Victorians (9)

For a full minute all the windows
In the east wall are your eyes

Sunrise never fails you see
In its diligence and infant glowing

Amphibrach of her and hair and clear
At the sun's innermost heart a cooing

My limited and abstracted art
Under every hedge finds sun

Finds a pebble likely to catch fire
Finds a child upright

Where lichen is a girl's and a boy's name
Rainbow rests

The sea has left us
But the sun remains

Victorians (10)

The sun is a forerunner of itself.
Picture a black road very early,
Desert mountains to the east,
No trees. As the sun rises,
Blacking then blazoning
The dry slopes, it also
Walks the road to you.

Truth like a canopy shelters truth,
Illusions of combat among the greenflies.
There is no sky. There is only the sun
And the sun's sharp progress
Through the Godforsaken, which is sunlight too.
I hear voices underneath the road.
Whichever way I go was once an ocean.

Victorians (11)

Also naked, misery gleams and is soon gone.
I hear, as if it were pebbles thrown
Against a metal awning, music from dreamland
Calling old misery, coaxing her eternal
Moon-blanched hoo-ha home.

And that leaves me. And that leaves you.
Beloved, choose any one you like of my alarms.
Make love to me on the fire escape.
In the apartment upstairs, the Aegean,
And in the one above that one, the North Sea
Ebb and flow.

Joy is the laundry drying on the roof:
Immaculate laundry, not ignorant,
But white and wise as the Sophoclean moon.

Homage to John Frederick Peto

1.

Fitfully in pictures disappearing now,
They are not toys but, rather, tiny horses
In the parade of youth: polish, spit and display
In fire companies throughout our country.

All in green we went out rioting.
Lute music damasked the commercial radio,
And girls knew everything.
Old friend, I remember your first wife.
She brought a loom into our world.
We turned the music up to drown its sound.

Now I am facedown in a disappearing picture.
I would know Christina Rossetti in a minute but not you.
Such is my skill set,
Blazon of a pathos soon abandoned.

2.

Muted extraordinary radiance,
Complicated if not impeded
By many things, most of them
In heaps where stone is stone,
Where wood is wood at close range,
Makes a fair portion of mind at midday
In desert mountains hard against my home.

Any ornaments for the poor man's store?
Any moments of leisure at the fish-house door?

14

I could show you rain just before the rain
And a black dog sniffing earthquake.
We die. Our children do not know us. We die.
I pray real prayers to a star too old
To climb these mountains up into the blue.

3.

A loop of string in the free-space otherwise,
And no, and more beautiful to see indigo
Buntings taking back the sky to me.

Littleness sometimes even resembling sunlight
Overflows with colors, with intervals
Like wingspans the wind drills of a Sunday.

To enter a flower is to find a child
Not one's own unharmed.
Our Lucie has a loop of string.

Time will come again to talk perfection,
A succession of creatures in midair.
I won't be there.

I've been given back the sky that was gone:
Five colors of rain, five new colors.

4.

Haphazard constellation of midges and old flowers
Blows through the garden shambles as slowly as the sun,
Vision somehow keeping time with itself so vision
Shows the kindness of a moment to the man
Seated beside roses planted here by his own hand

In the shade of a first heaven and the quick confidence
Of his humanity's evanescent song.

Creation's a funny word.
I think of noises rounding a corner
Becoming names, and then a child for each
Of the names climbs down the sun. Creation's the soul of
    haphazard.
I was old. I was young. I was old again.
Anymore Johnny, all I feel is fine.

"Jules Laforgue writes to say…"

Jules Laforgue writes to say you've died aboard ship
In the jeweled harbor of Montevideo.

Was it a dirty rifle or a broken cup
At rest upon the mirror's face he saw?

Efflorescence not a symbol, as simple
As reindeer swimming ashore in Uruguay

On Christmas morning. All symbols perish
At Christmas, and men are mute inside the newborn

Tides. The mirrors darken. Rifles will not fire.
The baby throws his cup against the pier,

And the pier collapses. Christ is alone.
The plague ships are forbidden the harbor.

Beauty for Beauty's sake and only later
For the sake of others, newborn for a day.

The Last Poem

A thousand happy mirrors are fighting to be seen.
—GRACE HARTIGAN

In the branches of North America
Monarch butterfly clings to an apple
In the rain for dear life

For a long time now I've tried to imagine
A steady diet of chrysalis—soup or stew
No matter, I only mean to eat the changes

The butterfly falls and drowns
And the chrysalis hunter with enormous hands
René Char lifts him gently to his mouth

There has been no poetry since Matthew Arnold
"Dover Beach" was the last and ever since
A good poem is purely the remembrancer of poems

I am dropping names along a swollen river
I am still reading and René Char eats
As he and I remember violins of foam and pebbles

Ice becoming leaves on the towpath
Ice becoming leaves on the towpath
It was music all the time if we knew

A perfect caprice on the wind and pigeons
Wheeling to the left of me I cannot die
There is a tiny woman in tall shoes pushing a stroller

Mexican I do believe she is made-up
To lead me to safety on mountain terraces
There is a God and she is the color

Keeping time to the caprice
Violins foam at her feet
The pigeons feed on monarchs too

II

BIRDS AND TREES

"The sky has slipped behind the moon…"

The sky has slipped behind the moon and the blue shows
    through
Blowsy flowers discarded propane canisters see
The moon dissolving not setting and the sun's immeasurable
Peace beginning now above the house

Little bird
Keep pace
With me
A while
And walk
I'm going
Only a little way farther on

Far back in my life an idiot complains of my philosophy
Light gives way to light all houses are magical
Little birds keep pace with every soul on earth

Pure

Stricken inside her heart a tree
And outside the wind clattering
Metal over stones
Where can she go
There's no silence to go to

Let me tell about vanity and a bee
Lady
Better to die inside a flower
Better to bind your soul in ice
And when you stand upright
Be a mountain Christ's footstool

I could not sleep last night for thinking
Mountain and stricken inside your heart
A tree

"You are the color not made..."

You are the color not made
Onto windows or white paper
Eight days' desert wind
Shifting quarter to quarter
With no pause leaves you shining
Along the black vein
Running from leaf to midday sun

I shall miss you when I die
And the sum of wisdom
Of eight days' desert wind
It is better to be young
Mending old trees than to be dying
Striving to bind a whiplash sapling
To wooden stakes

Aubade at the End

Soiled with blossom strange to say
Good earth and her cold creatures
Arise on wings and branches
For the man too weak to stand upright

Overnight is flowers
Cities and towns on stamens say
Overnight is flowers
There is one blossom so early now
It covers the sun's face

I cannot stand upright
Because there are newborn lights
Shaking the earth beneath me

One life one life and a broken tree is two trees
Mine a dead branch among the hundred living

"Moonlit cedar bursts in pain…"

Moonlit cedar bursts in pain.
Afterwards, even more stars shine.
The tawny-throated world is unharmed.
Even more stars shine.

Philomel is a nightingale
Because the world is no fit place
For human beings. We harm and ache.
Moonlit cedar bursts in pain,

Unharmed. I ask and ask again:
What brought me here? How do I stay?
American grass and Thracian wilderness
Grow peacefully with nothing to say,

Having fragrance, having palaces.
We are frivolous babies.
Still, I love a crowd of us. I rejoice
That the stars have not turned their backs on us.

Epithalamion

In sameness things
Reveal the differences
As in routine
Time's catastrophe
Unfolds unseen

Here is a tree
And ten years later
The same tree
Grows into death
The scent of love on it

The woman's shirt
Somehow today
Draped differently
Over our blue chair
Is clouds in the sky

Talons

Somewhere between Jew and free
Animal my Jesus makes a way
Narrow as the wind's space
In roses over thorns

Fig tree
Disappointed money-changer
Soul most of all a domestic animal
Dreaming at the soft edges of death
Wilderness when eagle means no harm
And prey adores
The perfect talons

Nothing follows any of those
Roses are torn and the wind
Passes through them all alone

"Pigeon dying in the box..."

Pigeon dying in the box I prepared
With grasses, water and a toy giraffe
For company, the angels here... but no,
We are alone and we are helpless.

Long ago, before the Great Lakes had their names,
Clouds hung in the air to think things through,
Choosing between the hazard of wings
And the certain but slow erosion of islands.

Pigeon, your wings are no good. As for me,
My island's worn to three stones and a puddle.
Here we are. Lake Michigan is Lake Michigan.
The fate of all beings is random and awful.

I have children out there. May some of them
Be lakes that climb into the sky and live.

What the Colors Mean

Evanesce a car an oriole
My life this very hour
Looses the words
Given wheels given wings
Given I won't be there
Although I lifted them once
Atop a wall to see the colors
And they told me what the colors mean

Green for green valley and red for happiness
The rest are secrets save for oriole
Which is a color in the afterlife

We say there is a bird on the branch singing
The branch itself is singing

Not even a breeze and yet the flowers tremble

Fedoras

Angelic patience, it rains to the ruin of spiders.

What use is a childhood? I never told
The warmest afternoon how daddy
Pulled the car over into a birch grove
Because the engine was failing. It had choked
On a dozen yellow birds, and we buried them.

Like the shadows beneath a stone bridge
Humans diminish towards midday. And then
We vanish. Fedoras. Polish sopranos.
The afterlife unravels before our eyes while angels
Cross the stone bridges back to Heaven.

I've been drunk ever since. The children
Have nothing to forgive, having never been children.
They buried no birds.

Pretty Alcoves

Houses so near and never entered
Years of increment or aggregate
Is it a thrasher on the nest
Is it a mockingbird how do we die
Alone never having lived alone
The trees have voices
The mockingbird and thrasher
Drive roots deep into the earth
Even flying and the woods burn

How we die
I have gone out riding every morning
Passing the dark doors and empty
Garden furniture in pretty alcoves
I don't know

Providence

Sparrows hopping around at all angles
And one becomes a little heap of flowers
In the shadow of my tilting tree.
Chide, chide the lowest branches.
The sun steps heavily, too heavily,
And Providence, Rhode Island, crackles into leaf.

You say that Shelley is dead. I agree,
Although in my sleep he ties a tricolor balloon
To a basket of small animals, up.
The sun is crippled, hence the fires.
Shelley hops away at an unusual angle.
What of the animals?

All beneath the tree in their balloon
They go underground, the envy of God.

Alsace

There are two skies but one hawk only
There are good days
And now that rain has filled the waste spaces
There is another

I have begun to learn in sleep that sleep
Plummets from the sky and makes
A screaming sound becoming solid
Becoming sapphires

The moon is hawk of the waste spaces
Screaming through his eyes

I had a good day and then another
I was married to mountains on all sides of me
The roads made Christmas very early
Mother sang to her hat same color as the car

"Mornings on a twig…"

Mornings on a twig
A finch's eyes God's eyes
Overflowing

Are those tears?

No, those are newborn stars

Aunt Patty chased the bee out of my bedroom
And so it was that I
Became an anthology piece
Translated along with many others
Out of the French into your small arms
Though I am a phantom

Are those your children on the stairs?

Yes, and they are angry with God
Who does not spare the finch but gives him eyes

"Birds small enough…"

Birds small enough to nest in our young cypress
Are physicians to us

They burst from the tree exactly
Where the mind ends and the eye sees

Another world the equal of this one
Though only a small boy naked in the sun

Glad day glad day I was born
Sparrow hatted old New York

And the physician who brought me
Drowned under sail next day in a calm sea

There are birds small enough to live forever
Where the mind ends and where

My love and I once planted a cypress
Which is God to us

City

Nevertheless a fragrance
One apple tree unmoved
Amid the bending tulips

Hello fat pigeon
I've come to an ending
Not a seashore after all
But one tree
Strange to me
Against familiar background annihilation
And other birds and the disappointment
In my son's eyes

I do not dream
Nor do I use my body
The way the rain does
Showing its dream into the shape of flowers

I only walk around
In pent April
Pavements cover the drab animals
And Noah's radiance

Rapture

Sparrow is footfalls
Cape of shadows
Shape of men
Where no men
Ought to be

Song comes after
Briefly if ever
In blind air

I have heard
Water where none
Was coolly going

I have seen
A sparrow becoming
The world's end

"A line of hills…"

A line of hills
Then a line of hills where the grass ends
And heat travels through trees
Into a happiness
Akin to the great happiness of imaginary children
Whitens the sky

How wonderful and final
My life becomes
The grit of the deathbed earth grows soft
A flight of swifts
Lifts an agate meadow to the sky

Kittenish alpine blown-apart dandelion
I have caught sight of my true friend
Rounding the hillside in his cloak of rain

III

TITHON

Shadows of leaves
Shadows of leaves
Je suis le prince
D'un pays aboli

God counts only up to one
His hands are small
And in God's hands even
Mountains are sparrow-sized

Also the cloistered fountains, Lord,
My dearest, my estranged,
The fountains also

Shadows of leaves
Shadows of leaves

A fountain at the axle of sunlight
And a child my child myself as a child waiting
In the shadows to enter the garden running
To plunge my hands in dazzling water

J'étais le prince
D'un pays aboli

My hands were as small as God's hands
In heaven sparrows
Became snows and cataracts around us
Creation is the miniature of creation
When God and I walked together we spoke paint

> *Then praises from the Mountains did arise*
> *As well as vapors...*   —TRAHERNE

Decades later my son and I were looking at museum pictures
X-ray a painting and behind the Ganymede you find
A crucifixion
X-ray a photograph and behind the napalmed children
Nothing
We spoke paint
Creation is irreplaceable
Ganymede again and again but never quite the same

The shadow of a leaf returns to the leaf
Dancing
When I was a prince each moment
Ventured outward
Returning to me covered in green leaves
I had a country I had a plan
At the center of creation
Dazzling waters would rise and fall
Small birds would sing in the leaves and small
Hands gather mountains into a ring
O my estranged, my dearest, the world
Can only be safeguarded by shadows
Dying unafraid into real colors
In your sunlight

> *...the happening/Of saints to their vision!*
> —DYLAN THOMAS

God is holding a mirror
No bigger than my eye
Beloved lost reciprocal
Restore to me
My infant eye

Will you read will you bring a color only one
Here to the mirror
White is water from which the colors rise
Touching the sunlight it becomes invisible
As in touching sunlight the eye goes blind
Becomes the empty mirror now as always
In God's small hand

An iridescent chaos —CÉZANNE

Green I can see when I see nothing
The green of a leaf makes love to its shadow
The dazzle is real it folds in upon itself
Vestige of rural remembered in the city of air
It folds in upon itself and the din of the birds is one note
Darkness gathers sex and color
My infant eye

Will you read will you live with me
In the city of first love all domes hovering
And the discarded stanzas capering
Like acrobats in the dark below the domes

First love is the love of God ignorant of God
A blinded girl her hands covered with paint
Touches me gathers sex and color
Both are one and each is the other
Adrift aloft in the infant mirror
Heaven gave me once to hold but I
Lived

> *The poem is always married to someone.*   —CHAR

I know the city is made of water not of wood
God sees
The blinded girl plunges her hands in
Heaven she can see
And the dome of the night sky is painted with clouds
Lovely living clouds

My words are painted with mouths
Clown costumes
Please think of me that way
Discarded tatterdemalion
Pleasured in the pitch-dark with a blind girl

The dome of heaven is a nest
It trembles and the nestlings
Fall into this world their mouths
Agape their mothers already gone
To God yet something
Is it death comes to gather them
Mends them and they arise
Singing their one note the green sound
Shaped by the updraft

> *There is a single leaf, in all this heaven.*   —AIKEN

Alone among the worlds ours
Is a paradise of discards
Broken from the beginning
We mend in death
Tumult dances a little at every shadow's end

The mothers are glad with God
As we are glad to be alone
Broken mirrors thrown into flowing water
Become souls
And the planet knows itself

13 August 2009

Dear Nathan,

It is the particular odor of God I love the most these days... a fragrance upon the edges of all things—leaves, a dragonfly's wings, scissors. It tells me that God is nearby, although I do not find him.

In a poem of mine somewhere (I looked through all my books this morning and never *did* find it), I wrote that each of the best minds ends by making fairy tales. And only yesterday, young friend, I received your beautiful manuscript. In it, every poem begins "Once upon a time," going on to tell a wholly new fairy tale fashioned out of Alabama ghosts and vivid children. Nathan, you have made a purest origin where I misplaced and badly misadventured the shadow of a leaf. I am nearby. I truly believe that I am near you there in Tuscaloosa, but do not look for me. I am better lost, and more helpful.

I think a lot of Cézanne these days and how, at Sunday dinner once, he rose from the table with tears over-brimming his eyes and said, "Balzac was thinking of me." Nothing more perfect! Nothing more poignant and irreplaceable! The irretrievable remembrance becomes a moment out of time, suddenly. And there you are, remembering stories yet to happen. What happens now?

Love,
Donald

> *Things aren't going well... Life is terrifying!*
> —CÉZANNE

A prince lay sleeping in his last adventure.
He dreamed a desert and saw three children there.
One by one they came to him for water,
Offering money, which he refused. To each
He gave an over-brimming bowl of cold,
Pure water. When they drank, the children
Turned to bone and ash. The prince slept on.

as if flowers were the point

The red tulips of Aix
Are gone the flowers
Cézanne himself would gather
By armfuls in between
Rows of ripening grain
Gone

The prince slept on. There were no children now,
And the desert was as dark as the small mirror
In God's hand. God held it close to the young man,
Capturing each breath as it was breathed,
Each dream of desolation. How wonderful,
How entirely human it is to dream the death
Of all creatures, leaving the planet to itself
In starlight. The mirror filled.
God stepped backwards into heaven. Once
Upon a time, the sun in the morning
Was painted like a mouth.

> ...*the child*
> *Ruling his god, as god intends he should.*
> —AIKEN

There is nothing in all this world nothing but one road

I lay my eyes upon the ground and see the ground
I lay my eyes upon a cloud (clouds are France) and see the
    angel there
I lay my eyes upon the slowly moving surface of the water
In a narrow pool between dragonfly and cruel acacia
And my eyes swim away from me finding my friends
Alive with skins made of diamonds (the poet Char) and high
    sounds (the poet Reverdy)
I lay my eyes upon the easternmost horizon just at dawn
And my only son Benjamin walks out of my eyes
Never to be seen by me

The shadows of leaves are addressed to immortality
Little birds give wings to the mountains and the mountains fly
Underground streams find a fountain cloister in New York
Nothing but one road in all this world there is nothing
But God myself alone as a child and counting
Up to one the garden number

Whistler's white girls disappearing into whiteness
Erotic toast
Is that what's wanted?
Inquire of my son who cannot sing
Inquire of my friends who cannot fly
Who in his right mind would burden
This wonderful creation with a consciousness?

> *Rousseau thought men good by nature; he*
> *found them evil and found no friend. Friendship*
> *cannot exist without forgiveness of sins*
> *continually.* —BLAKE

Who?

Dumb-shit absolute sovereign I love without limit
As I plunged my hands into your fountain body
And the mountains flew away into the noise of the shadows of
    leaves
I bit down upon the unreal underground God
You had no child to know
Erotic toast is what's wanted
And a prince beside himself with joy at the axle of sunlight
Knows that it is all hallucinations
And one of them is true

IV

THE AFTERLIFE

Made Mention

Fringe and halo
An hour is it
Or is it
All the ones
Come out of a black pail of smoldering branches?

Fringe and halo
The now forgotten
Cartoon elephants
And Utrillos show
More vividly than all
The best and rough-hewn I remember.

Love breathes deeply of the wood smoke.
Here is a rough-hewn table.
Here is a happiness with nothing underneath.
Love and another grope their way
Beneath the smoke along the drunken wall.

A roseate landscape glows in the quiet kitchen.
Take, dear one, into the keeping of your color,
These branches that were green an hour ago.

True Love

Out of doors eyes closed I must decide
Among trees the only one acacia willow locust
Bursting with the soupsweet noise of bees

Big morning tantivy big morning suicide
All night I was awake with useless sympathy
What use is childhood that falls to its death

Love makes us infamous
When love is coldly true

A man walks up a mountain and he walks
    halfway down
As for the rest he either flies or finds the body
    of Ovid
Broken open by a tree

Among all the clouds is only one that never moves
The world is singing to that cloud famously
True love true love true love

Barking Dogs

They are gabbing in three languages
Not one of them knows

Clematis is a fourth

And so the sun keeps still in its still agenda
Rusted underneath the broken swings
On soft earth

So many have come so far to play
Who cannot play who cannot
In this broken economy find a little shade to say

Clematis

Flowers were the bright detention colors
Young dogs bark and the flowers bark back

Let us be friends and not die
Let us mow the bright ground bare

Called

There is a heaven of disembodied voices and each
Knows Ibsen knows Central Park in late October
1969 it breaks hearts it is never
Silent and so it is I find myself
Weeping early May among Chinese
Bicycles headlong at the mountain's edge

Because of radio because the authors
Are not in eternity but here but invisible

I've seen no art only men and women
I can't explain it the men are too busy
Stealing and the tall the languorous Ophelias
Part a curtain in the rivers and disappear

No help at all but heaven still the same
Calls over distance the little words home

Forgiving Bells

The entire life of bells is a penance
Cast in iron by the makers, lest the barley
Fail to awaken, lest the believers
Come to grief in their unguarded fields.

Before the steeples, a baptism. Before
The bell-ropes, unction, an enormous
Linen alb and the murmuring priests.
A long afterlife of clangor and sometimes

Uncomprehending joy in the ponies
And treetops year after year atones
For iron-mongering mankind.
God is the sound when there is none.

And then the bells ring out and God goes.
Christ's hair in the hailstone melts away.

Rumors of Rain

The man is a cabin, poorly kept.
Outside, on the undulant ground, children
Loom, boulders at every point of the compass
But one, and each with weeds for its chapeau.

The woman, knowing her Ovid,
Is a bowl of apples indoors.
Forgetting her Ovid, she shapes
Her surface lights into the shape of breasts.

Humanness is a window thrown against a wall.
Better we were born inside of apples
And so remained. Rumors of rain
Would come to us in the little changes:

Withering or ripening, gold becoming
Crimson becoming a fine smile. The angel
Smiled exactly so when we were thrown
From heaven. The upper side of rain

With its battles and color, we still remember that.
And then the man pulled weeds from his warm pockets.
The woman stayed indoors, never to be seen
Again. Apples are a long way around,

And these are nothing to the hill of heaven.

Stag

With God not parted
But coming forward
As if through nets of frost
In the winter trees
Apple and birch and
Schumann's cinquefoil
Not even fifty years
No timpani
No drums of any kind

I lift my eyes
And my eyes
Teach me to roost
A secular bird
Ages and ages of lives
Garmented by God with nets
Of frost in a dream really
And snow of every kind
The drums were slowly falling
Through the cold darkening air

Stags are small
By which I mean to say
Each is a handful of snow
A gift from heaven's five-and-dime
Their hearts die into mine
Walking then dying
Our hearts together with God
Not parted as we feared
But going forward into apple trees
Girls visiting with flowers

I had an animal the only man
Who could describe the fragrance of a sound

"Faust cannot..."

Faust cannot, and all the nations
Become unreal, men and women so old,
No way to tell the difference anymore—
Only to love them, love them.

Oleander of this morning's drunkenness
Calls to the horses, who must not eat.
Radio music, yellow marimba,
Calls to Christ, who must not come again

Because I am enjoying the sunlight.
I am taking a respite from disgrace
To love imaginary deathless friends
Alive in these flowers

Where you will stay, please. I'll find you.
The color is youth.

"Out to the west..."

Out to the west
First moments of sunrise
Lightning
Black feathered lightning

Miss Curry left a harvest in the bed
A first home
All winter through
Rooms fell one by one into the street

Black feathered lightning angel of death
I do not think we shall keep our appointment
Dear Miss Curry we are both of us married
Disappointed not at all but crying

I've seen mountains racing from the sun
I've seen immortals and you are one

Winter Solstice

Slender moon a kind of scar or cicatrix
On the twilight sky
Harm's way

I remember there were stars on your wrist
One year ago
I counted them

A cavalcade

The world has a body and I have none
I go out walking and leave no mark
Out at twilight with the old moon
I leave no mark

A woman cannot know
The moment he is born
A man begins to disappear

"Unreal precision of the houses…"

Unreal precision of the houses at first light
45 years of rain and bodice
Grasses woods wildflowers
To be the only woman at this hour
Out in it one beauty one movie
And I am her hapless mule

Out of the blue one morning
My father took me north upriver
To see the mothball fleet
His war afloat and ghostly
Pennants of rain hanging from each spar
It's what we are

Discards of memory
Unreal until the only woman wakes

"Some motionless conflict in the sky…"

Some motionless conflict in the sky
As of Milton's angels painted there
In all their radiance and red malice

It is a special happiness and universal
Simply to know the names of colors
And to see them said

She mixed the colors for housepainters
That was New York Iowa Avignon
I'll take less luck if it means less stink she said

A special happiness
When clouds contest with clouds
In fixed flamboyance

Good versus Evil or beautiful cold hair
God loosed angels on us and they are the air

Last Man

The hawthorn is God's hat
And patterns in the marble
Swarm like bees

The world as I knew it would
Saunters out of the sexpool and lilacs
It begins to walk away

Little clodhopper
Crab apple numb with cold
Go quickly and take the buttercup
Keep pace with the sweet earth I cannot keep

I did not think the end would fall in the middle way
But I am happy now
That now is the hour
Even burrowing animals become creatures of the air

RECENT TITLES FROM ALICE JAMES BOOKS

Murder Ballad, Jane Springer
Sudden Dog, Matthew Pennock
Western Practice, Stephen Motika
me and Nina, Monica A. Hand
Hagar Before the Occupation | Hagar After the Occupation,
    Amal al-Jubouri
Pier, Janine Oshiro
Heart First into the Forest, Stacy Gnall
This Strange Land, Shara McCallum
lie down too, Lesle Lewis
Panic, Laura McCullough
Milk Dress, Nicole Cooley
Parable of Hide and Seek, Chad Sweeney
Shahid Reads His Own Palm, Reginald Dwayne Betts
How to Catch a Falling Knife, Daniel Johnson
Phantom Noise, Brian Turner
Father Dirt, Mihaela Moscaliuc
Pageant, Joanna Fuhrman
The Bitter Withy, Donald Revell
Winter Tenor, Kevin Goodan
Slamming Open the Door, Kathleen Sheeder Bonanno
Rough Cradle, Betsy Sholl
Shelter, Carey Salerno
The Next Country, Idra Novey
Begin Anywhere, Frank Giampietro
The Usable Field, Jane Mead
King Baby, Lia Purpura
The Temple Gate Called Beautiful, David Kirby
Door to a Noisy Room, Peter Waldor
Beloved Idea, Ann Killough
The World in Place of Itself, Bill Rasmovicz
Equivocal, Julie Carr
A Thief of Strings, Donald Revell
Take What You Want, Henrietta Goodman

ALICE JAMES BOOKS has been publishing poetry since 1973 and remains one of the few presses in the country that is run collectively. The cooperative selects manuscripts for publication primarily through regional and national annual competitions. Authors who win a Kinereth Gensler Award become active members of the cooperative board and participate in the editorial decisions of the press. The press, which historically has placed an emphasis on publishing women poets, was named for Alice James, sister of William and Henry, whose fine journal and gift for writing went unrecognized during her lifetime.

DESIGNED BY MIKE BURTON

PRINTED BY THOMPSON-SHORE

ON 30% POSTCONSUMER RECYCLED PAPER

PROCESSED CHLORINE-FREE

𝒸